HUMAN HABITATS

GUT

By
Robin Twiddy

Enslow
PUBLISHING

T0002041

Published in 2022 by Enslow Publishing, LLC
101 W. 23rd Street, Suite 240,
New York, NY 10011

Copyright © 2022 Booklife Publishing
This edition published by arrangement with Booklife Publishing

Cataloging-in-Publication Data

Names: Twiddy, Robin.
Title: Gut / Robin Twiddy.
Description: New York : Enslow Publishing, 2022. | Series: Human habitats | Includes glossary and index.
Identifiers: ISBN 9781978523562 (pbk.) | ISBN 9781978523586 (library bound) | ISBN 9781978523579
(6 pack) | ISBN 9781978523593 (ebook)
Subjects: LCSH: Digestive organs--Juvenile literature. | Gastrointestinal system--Juvenile literature.
Classification: LCC QM301.T95 2022 | DDC 612.3--dc23

Designer: Gareth Liddington
Editor: John Wood

Printed in the United States of America

CPSIA compliance information: Batch #CS22ENS: For further information contact Enslow Publishing, New York, New York at
1-800-542-2595

TRICKY WORDS

Bacterium = singular
(one bacterium)
Bacteria = plural (many bacteria)
Bacterial = to do with a bacterium
or many bacteria

Fungus = singular (one fungus)
Fungi = plural (many fungi)
Fungal = to do with a fungus
or many fungi

Photo credits:

4 - fun way illustration, ONYXprj, 6 - eveleen, Roi and Roi, 8 - inspiring, 10 - Yustus, 16 - 2018SENRYU, 18 - valeo5.

Images are courtesy of Shutterstock.com. With thanks to Getty Images, Thinkstock Photo, and iStockphoto.

All facts, statistics, web addresses and URLs in this book were verified as valid and accurate at time of writing.
No responsibility for any changes to external websites or references can be accepted by either the author or publisher.

CONTENTS

Words that look like <u>this</u> can be found in the glossary on page 24.

WELCOME TO THE HUMAN HABITAT

Hi! I'm Mini Ventura. My cameraman, Dave, and I have been shrunk down so we can make a nature documentary all about the tiny things living in and on us. Follow us into the human habitat — a world within a world.

Face

Lungs

Hair

Mouth

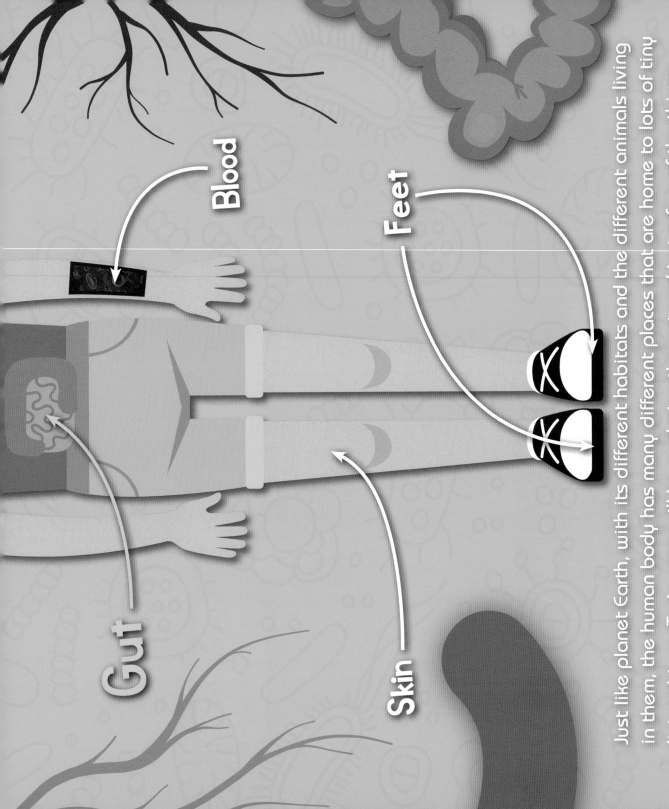

Blood

Feet

Gut

Skin

Just like planet Earth, with its different habitats and the different animals living in them, the human body has many different places that are home to lots of tiny living things. Today, we will be exploring the gut and just a few of the things living in it.

A LOT TO DIGEST

Gut is another word for the digestive tract. This is a long tube that runs straight through the body. The gut digests food. That means that it breaks it down and takes out the <u>nutrients.</u>

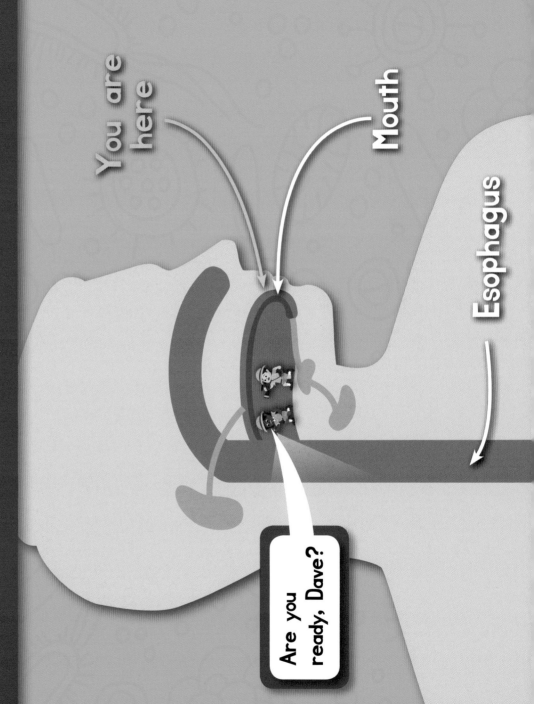

You are here

Mouth

Esophagus

Are you ready, Dave?

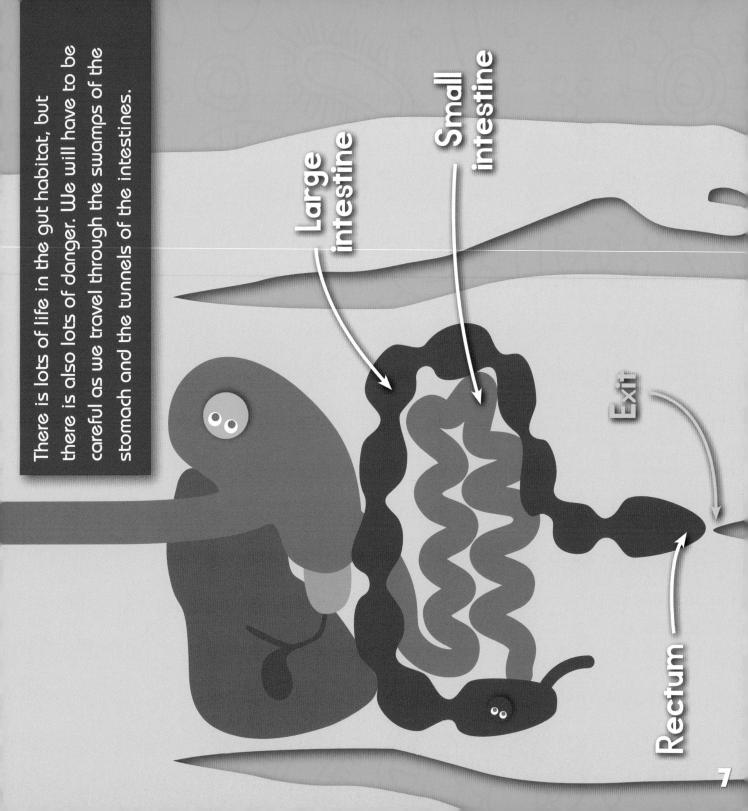

There is lots of life in the gut habitat, but there is also lots of danger. We will have to be careful as we travel through the swamps of the stomach and the tunnels of the intestines.

Large intestine

Small intestine

Exit

Rectum

THE ESOPHAGUS: IT'S ALL DOWNHILL FROM HERE

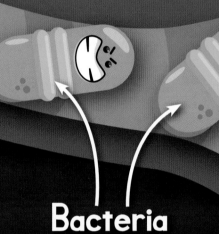

Bacteria

This is the esophagus. Food from the mouth is swallowed and enters here. The esophagus squeezes and pushes the food down toward the stomach.

Look at all that <u>bacteria</u>. It's quite normal to see bacteria in the esophagus. Some of it comes from the mouth and is quite friendly.

It is pretty squishy in here.

It's a tight squeeze, Dave.

Esophagus wall

SURVIVING THE STOMACH

Something called a <u>mucus membrane</u> covers the walls of the stomach. This stops the stomach <u>acid</u> from burning through the stomach.

Here in the stomach, food is <u>churned</u> up and broken down by the stomach acid. It is warm and moist – the perfect habitat for bacteria and <u>fungi</u>. So where are they all?

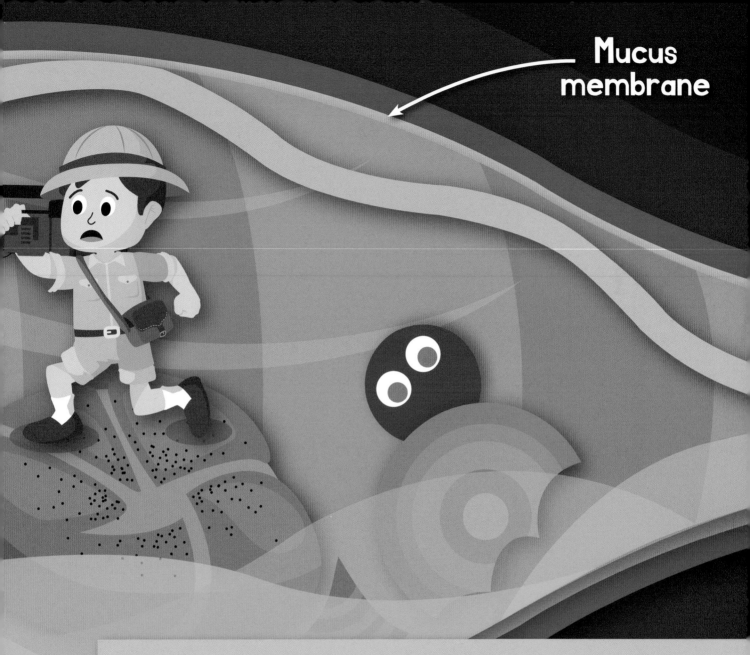

Mucus membrane

There are some bacteria living in the stomach, but the acid used to break down food makes the stomach uninhabitable for most things. Uninhabitable means impossible to live in.

THE DIGESTION CONNECTION

Uh-oh! Things are going to get a little messy in here. The human habitat has swallowed some food. Look – the stomach acid is rising, and the walls are moving to slosh it all around.

This sloshing and breakdown of food makes it ready for the next part of its journey into the small intestine. If you look carefully at the food, you might see some new bacteria from outside.

See, this is why no one wants to live in the stomach!

The stomach acid will take care of those invading bacteria. Quick, Dave — into the small intestine!

SMALL INTESTINE

This is the small intestine. It is long and dark and full of bacteria. There are some good bacteria in here that help the small intestine get the nutrients out of the food.

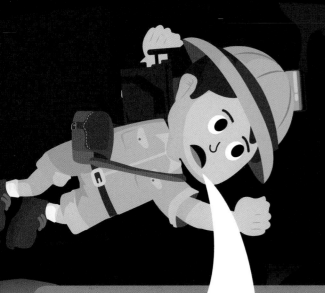

Phew, that was close. I didn't think we were going to make it out of the stomach in one piece.

We'd better get moving. It is a long way to the large intestine!

The small intestine is guarded by an army of <u>white blood cells</u>. They try to stop bacteria that might harm the habitat if they get in.

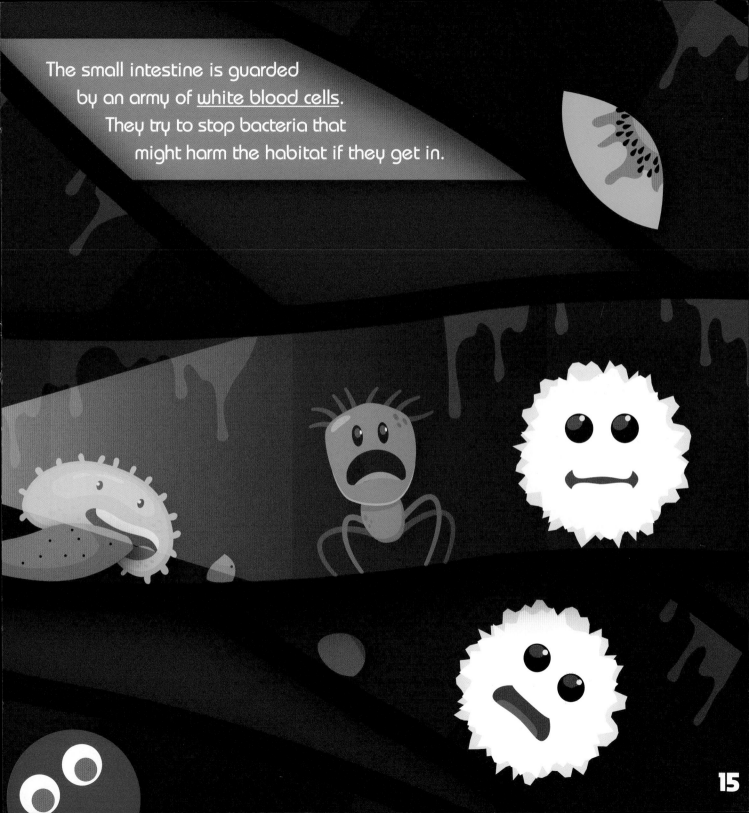

LARGE INTESTINE

Here in the large intestine, there are a huge number of bacteria. Billions and billions of them are here, waiting to digest the food even further. As the bacteria work at removing the last nutrients, they make a strong-smelling gas.

It doesn't look much like food anymore.

The large intestine sucks most of the water out of what was once food. When it reaches the end of the large intestine, it will be more solid and <u>familiar</u>.

The smell is getting really strong in here. I think it is time to find an exit.

STOPPED BY THE SPHINCTER

Oh no! The sphincter is closed. The sphincter is a type of door made of <u>muscle</u>. We need to get out of here before the <u>stool</u> is ready to leave the habitat and push through that door.

I hope this thing opens soon.

SURPRISE PARASITE!

The sphincter is opening, and it leads to another sphincter. Wait, what is that blocking the way? It's a tapeworm! Tapeworms can live up to 30 years and grow up to 82 feet (25 m) long — that is about twice as long as most buses!

I just need to get a picture of this tapeworm for my parasite collection before we move on.

Tapeworms <u>absorb</u> food through their skin. Their heads have hooks and suckers to help them hold on in the bowels when they are getting sloshed around.

RUMBLE RUMBLE, BYE!

We have arrived at the final sphincter. This one leads outside. Our journey through the damp tunnels of the gut has been hard and smelly.

We have learned a lot about the bacteria that live in the gut. Not all of it is bad. In fact, some of it helps the habitat digest food. Wait, what's that noise?

GLOSSARY

absorb	to take in or soak up
acid	a chemical that can break things down
bacteria	tiny living things, too small to see, that can cause diseases
churned	moved around quickly and with force
documentary	a film that looks at real facts and events
familiar	already known and recognizable
fungi	living things that often look like plants but have no flowers
habitat	the natural home in which animals, plants, and other living things live
mucus membrane	a covering on the walls of the stomach that creates mucus
muscle	a bundle of tissue that can contract or squeeze together
nutrients	natural things that plants and animals need to grow and stay healthy
stool	the solid waste from a human body
white blood cells	parts of the body's immune system, or defense system

INDEX